Darwin's Mother

INSTITUTE *of* **Museum** *and* **Library** SERVICES

"Celebrating Ohio Book Awards & Authors 2020" was made possible in part by a grant from the Institute of Museum and Library Services. CFDA 45.310, Project #VIII-70-20

SARAH ROSE NORDGREN

PITT POETRY SERIES * ED OCHESTER, EDITOR

UNIVERSITY OF PITTSBURGH PRESS

Published by the University of Pittsburgh Press, Pittsburgh, Pa., 15260
Copyright © 2017, Sarah Rose Nordgren
All rights reserved
Manufactured in the United States of America
Printed on acid-free paper
10 9 8 7 6 5 4 3 2 1

ISBN 13: 978-0-8229-6516-9
ISBN 10: 0-8229-6516-X

Cover art: Julie Heffernan, *Self-Portrait as Great Scout Leader*, 1998. Oil on canvas, 74 × 60 in. Reproduced with the permission of the artist.

Cover design by Joel W. Coggins

To know what things can come about, and what cannot arise,
And what law limits the power of each . . .
—Lucretius, *The Nature of Things*

I'm a brilliant machine
Composed of softer things
—Sylvan Esso, "Jaime's Song"

CONTENTS

Darwin's Mother

GHOST LESSONS

All winter the ghosts were waiting
for a high school teacher who

refused to appear, and so you
were roped in. February

had paused the year, the days
like holes that tripped you over

and over in the frozen yard. You had
no knowledge of history or chemistry

yet were expected to teach
the dead from a colorful handbook,

diagrams resembling medieval castles
or cells. This chapter illustrated

how every nucleus requires
fortification, the tender ward

and inner structures bounded
by bright blue membranes.

But no amount of learning, the students
told you, had brought them closer

to the master they all loved—the invisible one
who had no use for books

or the offerings of bread his many
admirers left for him

at the door of the school.
They all watched his empty chair

with awe. His absence took up half
the room. The only proof

they had to show you was
a tidy pile of clothes and hair

like the fur and bone an owl
coughs up after feeding. Such dire love!

But, they said, don't pity us. Everyone
must spend their lives devoted

to a magnificent person
who can feel nothing for them.

Origin of Species

A REPORT FROM OUR TEAM IN THE FIELD

We have discovered a monster
in bits and pieces, bones
we chisel from rock it took millennia
to form, and millennia again
to remove grain by grain by tweezer
and brush. We toil in shifts
to extract her. Our cutting-
edge instruments, furnished
by the University in their liberal
support for our prodigious efforts,
shine. A complex creature,
she is headless, all body, daily
exiting the mountain in a slow
trickle of limbs and digits (heart
and lungs and belly long gone)
we fill our satchels with. Yes,
she is dispersed and has allowed
this incremental carrying
away, a continuous gifting
and diminishment. But far from
generous, she insists on holding
back from us, resisting our tools
and our innocent task that
will surely lend fame to her.
Each movement brings a little pain,
so she stiffens against the inevitable
disclosure, increasing her own difficulty
like any young, laboring mother.
So, we work not only despite
the rock but the beast's rigidity also,

her panic as we unlatch time. We admit,
some days it's hard to maintain
a neutral heart regarding
the outcome of a job that's never finished.
Our department is unwavering
in its faith, yet our wives tire
of the local market's measly
choosings, the rough society here.
Still, be assured of the team's confidence
that we'll fulfill our purpose
and collect sufficient data to prove,
finally, our own worth even
against her evident greatness.
Even if she did, in essence,
give us birth, we believe our race's
proportions to be superior both
in function and form (though
it's true the coupling
of refinement with brute strength
found in items A-16 through A-25
are impressive—an unparalleled
marriage of opposites
which may appear perfect
to the untrained eye).

MITOCHONDRIAL EVE

Please go down and thank her
under the arched branches
where she sits on her heels

arranging a circle of leaves
for a good bed. And on the inside
of her skin thank the mosaic.

Take what little she has and
give it back—one piece
and another, marked with plastic

tags. How high can she count
from your sieves submerged
in water sorting her shards

that lay a mosaic over the earth?
You know the entry when
you see it, in fact

you'd recognize her anywhere—
Reclining in pain on her bed
under a mile of boulders

always with the door open.

DARWIN'S MOTHER

He lolled on her belly like
a piglet on a sow, his skin
caked in white paste.

A draft lifted her
ruffled collar, and Darwin's
mother's memory of pain

was just now seeping
out of her. He was taken away
and then, in a moment,

placed back in her lap, prim
and dry. Newly civilized
in lace and linen.

She recoiled in sullied
silk and ribbon when she first
saw his face: In a way, he was

already a man, therefore
discomfited by the smell
of her good clean blood.

DR. HARRY HARLOW'S PRIMATE LABORATORY

University of Wisconsin, 1958

I was cut down like a fruit
before they hauled me with the others
toward a town of skinny trees.
In the back of the van
I looked down and found myself

separate from the other bodies.
It was a nice, sharp feeling
and I tested it by kicking
my arms and legs sharply
all the way to the clinic where I lived
the first few weeks. I pleased
the men by letting them take

their mms and ccs. And as a gift
I was given a wire mother
and cloth mother to choose between.
The wire one held the milk

but I was drawn to the feeling
of the cloth on my skin.
Neither of their faces moved.

This is a message for my brothers
and sisters who may follow me
from a long way off: Between
the two kinds of hunger
there can be no question.

AN UNCONTACTED TRIBE

We fly over the jungle
in a metal machine, thinking nothing
special of it—green, so much
green. The camera's powerful
zoom lens allows us to film
from more than a kilometer away, causing
minimal disturbance to the tribe
the government denies exists.
And we can peer anonymously
through the lens, that portal
where now our close-up bird's-eye view
sweeps over the expanse, the canopy
like velvet concealing stolen
watches, the vendor beginning to expose
his wares gleaming in a clearing.
Maybe they're covered more
like genitals than jewelry, actually,
since their bodies are hot and soft, caked
in red paint they make from the seeds
of the annatto tree, not fashioned
from disparate parts.

They appear in twos and threes, faces
upturned for the plane's flybys.
They can hear the engine's
weird drone and see, what? A white
bird reflecting sun off its back?
A demon? At the edge of the trees, standing
guard before their low grass huts
and gardens of manioc and papaya,

one kneels and draws his bow
while the others seem awed—
they stand so still. Certainly, we
are awed because their bodies
light the jungle like red candles
with black flames, like fingers
counting one and one and one.

Jose, whose job it is to keep
their location secret, says filming is the best way
to protect them, to prove they're real.
And so the camera *captures* them,
lifts their bare feet from where they meet
the soil, sucks their bodies up
through air, into the airplane's open door
and through the lens like
blood-colored dolls. We eat
the sight of them whole.

THE WEED

The weed wants so much
to hurt like an animal

but it is simple
and can only keep track

of one goal at a time. An ugly
and agitated shadow circles it—

it is the horses stamping
in a cloud of flies

their swarmed eyes
lashed by the others' tails.

I am always becoming
as you need me to be,

says Jesus, and the weed
may as well say it, too.

Like lovers finishing
each other's sentences

the two have grown
inseparable.

They even dress alike
these days, since each

has sheathed one of his many
blades in tender purple.

DARWIN'S MOTHER

In God who formed one body
after another in my middle

like the red speck growing in a yolk
to fill the egg with feathers
and folded bones
                    lies perfection.

And in the fragile egg, its shell
weak and broken open
like chips of sky, fine pottery,

breathes a red and fluttering clot
prone to illness and sin.

Like God, I give birth to men
so they might build a church
and a government over me,
making it easy for me
                    to become

transparent, a strip of gauze
hung over a side chair or pinned up
in the chapel or garden
so the silhouettes of columbines
will show through my skin.

IGUANODON

On New Year's Eve in 1853 at the Crystal Palace in London, prominent scientists attended a banquet held inside a life-sized mold of a dinosaur.

She looks, from a distance, like
roadkill—glassy-eyed and frozen
with her hollowed torso
open to the air—or a dish

to fill with night. They've erected
wooden posts to hang a canopy
and pinprick chandelier
so tomorrow, after

the speeches, they'll see across
the grounds a cocoon of light
as they approach her in ties
and tuxes, flutes chiming.

Up close, it's instantly clear
her death, even, is pretense.
The nearest she'll ever be
to breath—except in resemblance

to the prehistoric animal
she imitates—is the stretch of evening
her makers will inhabit her, a dining
table where her spine would be

and the men, like ribs, protruding
from each side. She could dream
the whole thing: violins singing
and the best of Science smiling within her

as their small, square teeth
pull meat from silver
tines, her spaciousness,
what revelry, a bulging hum

in her gut, how she contains
two vast moments at once
without flinching. Though
her feet are bolted down

and her head is full of clay,
when the music starts she'll know
it's time. *If only*, she thinks,
my ghost were here to see it!

BREEDERS

Annie Darwin (1841–1851)

My father and I love pigeons because
of the many ways they might go wrong:
No appetite, watery droppings, air
in the crop, swollen eyes, or unable to eat corn.
Some have tail feather cases that don't open.
Last year we had baby fantails whose crops
became filled with a white substance
and who died unless we squeezed them out.
And now this two-week-old roller bird won't
hold his head upright. He walks
backward with his eyes partly closed, but
he eats well and his droppings are fine.
My baby brother is like that—no tension
in the muscles. When father orders
the ten of us by height on the low bench,
no two of us have the same complaint
and we are soft as birds. Some of us are pretty,
some limp, some have lighter hair,
but we all love to be pitied and nursed.
Each of us is an experiment, but I'm
my parents' favorite because my sickness
hasn't a name. Most of us will live past ten,
the others buried under mounds
in prim boxes. Lined up like this
we eye each other, and our eyes
link together in a light blue chain.

THE ANATOMIST

Gaslight shuddering in a glass globe,
pen dipped into a black hole,
and a line-drawing as he writes in the labels
so we know the book is to be about sex.
Until then, we misread the clues. Maybe
when the figure waits on the paper
the way she feels is universal, a general
sense of being carefully observed.
But when he adds the words we recognize
her from the diagrams at school
that made us blush. This goes in here
which receives it thus. This lights this
with a white flame. This opens. This grows.
This is what soft and hard feel like. This
plants a seed in the earth. This gives.
This makes the world. Accidentally,
his ink leaks over the surface, blotting the line
between her and the outside.

MOTHER, PRESSED

She instructs me in her vacant way
to identify the flower

by looking inside the blossom—
deep inside the blossom

to spy its waxy alchemy,
the sight of its pink

skirt and pointed yellow feet
flattened between two sheets

of translucent paper,
while at the same time

butterflies vie for her hair,
my shirt is stained

by pollen, her bosom
looms above my head

and a thought deep inside
the sun whites her face out.

DARWIN'S MOTHER

The door at the top of the stair,
a black velvet gown,
her curiously constructed

worktable, deathbed—
these are all I remember
of my eighth year,

since after my sisters' grief
placed coins on our lips,
her name disappeared.

VIRTUS ET SCIENTIA

Perhaps it was a mistake to make
our motto Virtue—our one
virtue being to need the very least.
We ask so little while other teams
receive write-ups and cold weather gear.
It's not that we don't submit
requests to our supervisors,
we make them most neutrally
and on the proper forms.
But our ink is the exact color
of our paper, and the local post office
indefinitely closed. By now
we've learned to live on so little,
even our hearth fires are frugal.
We feed them the same brittle sticks
our specimens imitate in both field
and glass case, since they can't
discern between the two. After years of
making do, we are embarrassed
to have wanted at least some small
applause for our suffering—
That is the secret wish we hold
like a white candle among us all the time.
Our specimens respond with less
and less enthusiasm to external stimuli.
We maintain our notes, but Progress only
inches forward on its hundred frail legs.
Numbers for degrees of movement.
Numbers for degrees of stillness.
Feelings have very little to do with it.

LIFE WITHOUT A SPINE

*Taxonomists have described more than a million species . . . divided
into more than 20 phyla. Of this plethora, vertebrates represent
only part of one phylum, and a mere 40,000 species or so.*
—Stephen Jay Gould

Try to imagine your entire body as a face
and your mind a color, an electric
secret kept even from (especially from) you.

But we want to think about terrestrial life—
we're like this great museum muralist
who blotted out sea creatures and insects

once the vertebrates appeared. We'd rather gaze
at reptiles that run like dogs, and mammals
trundling towards us in a great *progression,*

than conceive of the underwater mindflowers
floating oceans covering (to this day)
seventy percent of Earth's surface.

Even now, I whose language breathes
my mind out in airy tendrils, I
diminish them by pointing my finger bone.

Material

MATERIAL

Yes, we have a soul. But it's made of lots of tiny robots.
—Giulio Giorello

My soul rose up in me,
a colony I follow.
My soul has a trillion brittle wings,
a billion black bodies.
My soul formation is Stratus.
My soul's parts know little
and don't care whether I live or die.
Its components make a mind outside of me,
hovering over the driveway.
My soul is not waiting—
It cannot wait.
What is the sound of my soul?
Incessant clicking and chattering
like many sets of tiny, wind-up teeth.
It appears as a hurricane,
sandstorm, or soot billowing.
Its moveable parts can arrange themselves
to make a mechanical hand.
My soul pulls at my soul.
I am not responsible for my soul
for it acts independently.
I am in awe of its cities
and public works.
Its vast demolition projects.
Every seventeen years
my soul disperses after mating
and litters the road
with fat, crushed zeros.

RESERVOIR

It is the nature of data
to pool in low places. Sometimes
it cuts the land in two

like a river. Other times it falls
over deserts unpredictably, moved
by an unseen wind.

It takes a staff of thousands
traveling on foot with tin buckets
under their arms to collect
even a fraction of it, emptying it all

into the reservoir we're building
for this very purpose.

At 130,000 square miles,
the reservoir is not much smaller
than the state of California.

When it's filled, skilled workers
will set about manually separating

the data into troughs.
For example, information related
to weather will be extracted

from medical records
and school attendance, and all of these
divided from personal emails.

How tidy it will be before the experts
find a use for all this information!
Tourists outfitted in protective clothing
will pay to peer into

the lake of digital blue,
the infinity of opaque surfaces
refracting sunlight
that will light their faces

as they stare and say, My God
how beautiful.

PILLAR OF FIRE BY NIGHT

There is a black side
and a white side of sleep
knitted up the center
in a column keeping
watch over you, traveler,
asleep in your hut.
The white side gathers
all your breaths
and funnels them into
the great lung outside
your body, calling forth
and forcing back a stream
of air. The black side
is the pilot light burning
in the earth three feet below
your cot. The low-down
tug of heat. How long will you
lie there with the miles
pulled tight in your sheet?
A *little sleep, a little slumber,*
a little folding of the hands to rest.
I see you from above
and at a distance west,
your hut among hundreds,
while the pillar
pluming over camp
rifles your notebook,
your ledger pages.

CICADA

For four years my daughter
has been sleeping among the other
daughters. She nurses
in her sleep like the others too,
sucking tree roots and turning
her black head down
in the dirt. My daughter waits
to be chosen deathlike,
indistinguishable from the brood
in her lacey bunting with eyes
shut tight. I waited like her
back when all of me fit
in a walnut and Darwin's daughter
lay on the grass dreaming
a daughter's dream with her ankles
crossed. Under her body
underground, we hundreds
of daughters envied her weight.
We felt her above us like a mother
though she was only another
daughter. And then the next month
she stopped breathing and went
all dry and veiny like a wing.

THE CELL

After the cell's life goes out, she might turn
just the perfect color and link
herself into a strand of hair.
Or, depending on her assignment,
she could lie trampled on the wet
forest floor all winter
until one morning I walk past and
don't notice she's decomposed.
She could hold her sisters
above her on a long stalk. Otherwise
she's consumed by them—
all evidence destroyed. She serves
the faith behind the word.
Speaks a yes or no language, a code
that translates either as *die* or *don't die*
quite yet. She is the best listener
in the world. She composes
the world. The switch flips one way
and she grows out of nowhere, tiny
mass in a larger body. Then
she hears the signal and
switches back off automatically—
a TV screen or floodlight.

FLY

There are two kinds
of threads in this world:
the smooth, radial ones

the spider stands on and
spins from, and the sticky,
parallel ones that catch the flies.

The gridding is the exact
size of the fly's black motor.
The threads are invisible.

Taking measure, the mother
stitches her unborn's
clothes. She sews *something*

excessive, something *lowly*.
It will fit him perfectly.
Headfirst and clumsy, he

comes on a drumroll of wings
til he's borne into
the *properties of lifeless things.*

TICK

Small island of senses,
lifeworld in which you are
blind, deaf and dumb,

guided by warmth as you
crawl upward, the light
playing its melody

on your skin, then
the smell of butyric acid
as you fall into
                    a provisional totality,
as you fall into being.

The warmth of the animal
triggers you to suck,
so you suck the heat

into yourself, the universe.
Your blindness, armor.
Your deafness, the space

inside song, til you grow
contrapuntal to the mammal,
a composition, *faultless.*

PREGNANCY

For Brita

There is a spark
in your body.

You mark it
with a red star.

Other colors follow for
other ailments,

but mostly
it's water and fire.

You melt the crayon
down again. Water. Fire.

Holding the paper
still with your hand.

But still
it's hard to find the center since

the outline drowned.
That spark is a bleeder

and takes your body over
part by part. A fleck

in the deep
bowl of grief you grew from.

BLUE POEM

Cloud, steam and smoke. River, ocean and lake. Water, and its tight path through the granite slab. It all moves down to the basin and back, clean or full of foreign matter. The air is its mirror, so the whole world's stuck in a clamshell forever.

Glass, beaker and gauze. Ink, knife, needle. Light, which is indefinite until dismembered in a chamber. The drink stains your insides so the machine can see them. You slide right under.

THE OUTER CRUST

The outer crust of my life peeled away
and under it I am left with a white
and trembling egg, round as the moon.

Wounded also, in those places where the flesh
had sealed to the shell
and came away with my thumb.

Gradually, the surface solidifies.
Soon it will grow hard again and begin
giving off dust. To hold it

is to hold a pebble from another planet.
To throw it is to watch it grow
further and further away each year

by a worm's length.

BEHIND MY BRIGHT EYE

Behind my eye
a little door leads to a loose
copy of Earth

suspended in pink
liquid. Like bits of paper

brain tissues cling and fall apart
when you reach in
your finger.

On the wisps are
trees, animals, cars.

This version will last longer
than the real thing
but, still, not forever.

When putting it together
the maker should've planned
for what the ruins will look like
in the distant future—

a snow globe
flurrying, but with stars
instead of snow.

THE NETWORK

To you, the group we speak for
may seem loosely specified,
but the members fall
under many of the same categories
indicated by our program.
We like to imagine these members
living together in one blue circle
projected on a white wall,
much like the traditional families
we know of from history.
We chose this image of the blue circle
because it communicates the group's
unified stance toward the public
as well as a cool, calm feeling
like looking down into an alpine lake
that grows or shrinks in proportion
to the number of fish living within it.
In this way, the program mostly runs itself
after the initial install. A series
of graphs broken down by members'
interests can be envisioned
on the opposite wall,
but we prefer focusing on the simple
blue circle which, in addition to the ideas
we already mentioned, also represents
memory—a necessary addition
to any true community.
We've learned a lot about community
since we took this job back in 2004
and there are some common

misconceptions. First of all,
groups don't actually have anything
they want you to say for them. The job
is more about watching patiently
until you know what they want to hear.

THIS VALLEY

Dark fire burns down
in the tar swamp and weather waits
for more info to come in.

Weather has learned from experience—
fire cannot be trusted;
she needs time and data

to determine her next move.
Because they are sisters,
weather believes she can often

predict fire's behavior.
She is wrong this time:
fire reduces to a smolder

instead of flaring up.
In response, weather cools
and rolls out a cloud cover

which in turn affects horses,
flowers, grubs, and such.
Weather is everything to us,

but to her we are just blips in the throat
as she goes on breathing
her zeroes and ones.

ANIMAL SPACE

The bush sings brightly by
the lane, dispersing
its hundred cheeps to the air.
Behind the leaves you can see
many birds hung
through a vast, enveloping network
like the scientist who,
after treatment, gained depth
perception for the first time.
While walking home
from teaching at the university,
she was amazed by the opening
of the trees which now held
"pockets of space" between the leaves,
and in winter by how she was now
a part of the voluminous
snowfall instead of just watching it
on a movie screen like she'd done
her whole life. The proportions
of animal space grew around her head
so now she could locate her deep
ancestors, as well as those relations
who never were—every one
of Earth's species surrounded by a cluster
of possible monsters. She saw
the real animals dotted
here and there throughout the air,
but fell in love with those hypothetical ones
who hovered at their real shoulders
like an entourage of angels.

A Moral Animal

ABOUT US

We have some things in common.
Like, we are in love
with each other. We all went to the same
high school, but graduated
in different years. We are loyal
to a television show about a hospital.
We are bereft. Our skin prickles
for the cool, firm hand
of the doctor, his stiff white
cuff and steely tools. We offer
each other little, and receive little.
We insert pennies to be stamped
with our emblem. We are like nurses
who have fallen ill ourselves, still
dressed in blue. We are against
the regular patients who must be washed
and scattered. We can go
at any time but choose not to. We thrive
among clatter and order. So clean
we could eat off each other.
We watch our favorite program
from adjustable beds. We Share photos
of our families poolside in Barbados.
We Like pictures. We dream
of filling the high school auditorium to see
our favorite band playing just for us.
We stand close enough to speak
electrically. We have very sensitive skin.

THE KISS

Ready to absorb any insect
who lands on them, red hairs
arrange themselves on a long leaf.

The Sundews take shallow,
hovering breaths from their clear

globes along the windowsill
where I feed them
distilled water through a straw.

Tonight, you and I are here
in this dream kitchen. We're trying

to boil tea for our dinner,
but trapped in the glass kettle,
an enormous fly bumps around
like a meaty fist.

You put your mouth over the steaming
spout and suck his body out,

holding him somewhat crushed—
his feet and wingtip poking from
your lips—but you don't bite down.

So the kettle is clean. But now
if I want to kiss you (and I do),

this iridescence, dead
and black and shining—

MORAL ANIMAL

My desire was greater than any other
person's desire, but I was connected
to all other people through it.

I abstracted it from the particulars
of my life so others might
recognize it close to home.
Free from those false details I found it

taking its own shape but still
stuck to me in places like a falcon

on fresh tarmac struggling to fly. I wanted to
free myself from it too since
I was now the most limiting factor
but was afraid I wouldn't survive the hurt,

or that I'd become unrecognizable
to people I knew. If I didn't act
however, ligatures were threatening
to pull me across a threshold
I hadn't chosen. That was all yesterday.

This morning I find myself
in more or less the same dilemma
except perhaps resolved to
do the wrong thing. This makes
my desire cooler and more compact

with a weight similar to regret
or a goose egg. I'm able now to place it

near me on the table while I read.
Off and on it rotates slightly
and I feel my posture shift slightly.

ACHILLES AND MARY AT THE MUSEUM

1.   Lady, let me touch the white
plaster of your dress. Let me cup
your two hard mounds then tightly wrap
my hands around your waist.
I want to slip my fingernails
under the flaked paint
of your starry mantle. Make
an impression of one golden curl
like a nautilus on my palm,
so I may carry it with me forever.
Please allow me to be familiar
as I grip the flat stump
of your missing right arm.
Most excellent lady, might I
be bold enough to pierce your eyes
which, in prayer, you have cast down?

2.   Like a salmon in midair, like a deer
or a beacon, like a sapling
stripped but still standing, like
a heavenly flame, your nakedness
burns the atmosphere. Shape
like the sky wrapped tight around
a pencil, an expanse shored up
and sanded down to the smoothest
material. Your brow's tender angle
shows you are young—like me,
you will always be young. If I could
look behind your shield I might see
that your heart was torn by the tip
of a spear. And below that, how time
broke your sex from its nest.
Your fingers lift as if to ask some
question, but the two of us forever
stand five, or maybe six, feet apart.

ELECTROMAGNETIC

If separated on either side
of a barrier, two live heart-cells

will sync and beat in time.
And the deer all winter

follow each other
past your kitchen window

every evening—one
venturing first and the others

trailing in line. "Too bad
technology has overridden the soul

and we can no longer experience
true thinking. Not even

the President has power
anymore." You share this fact

with the doctor who is monitoring
your heart. He could

perform an ECG from three feet
outside your chest if needed,

the electromagnetic force
of the organ is that strong. "Really,"

he says, "our hearts could
each power a small light bulb." "Now

that would be a useful technology,"
you say dryly, "But seriously,

there's no escape from all this
madness but to abandon the whole

doomed ship of modern culture
and move off to the jungle."

A return to primitive, *real* life.
Fruit and sex and weather

and genuine work. Illness
could be mystical again.

You could even sleep out
under the glorious stars where

a snake the exact diameter
of your throat would find you,

crawl in through your mouth
and devour every system.

SIMULATION

July 21, 1969

Admit it: Your whole life there's been a remove
between you and greatness, between you
and disaster. In this middle place
light waves make the living room furniture
visible, and your son in his striped pajamas
testing gravity down there on the circular rug.
Your eyes and ears hover
some distance above the couch as he positions
carefully one foot before the other.
When your hand makes contact
with the glass of Coke sweating on the table,
what you feel is a slick surface, not the vast
space inside each atom, which is like
the space around an orange suspended in the center
of a football stadium. Time shifts
in flickers while the world keeps happening
inside a box you can only look into.
It's all there behind the screen: earth receding
into blackness, and, as a man makes tiny bootprints
in dust the color of gunpowder, a collective
breath of relief from mission control.
Reassuring and paternal at his desk, Cronkite
pulls you in, "Because if we are not able
to land"—he must be addressing you now—
"at least we are able to follow."

MOVIE NIGHT

Easter Sunday, and it's just
the two of us here
on the guest cabin's sofa where
no one would think to look for us.
We've been reenacting
our favorite horror film from the 70s,
the one in which my baby
climbs out from the deep
slice in my abdomen too early,
and I hold you still
attached by your cord
through the cut that split me in half
like a gourd. You try to nurse,
but my mother on the telephone says
you'll never get what you need
out here in the air. The rest
of the film follows me
as I wander through McDonald's
screaming for a clean sink.
It's an emergency. I have to rinse
the urine off of you before
my hands can spread apart
all my wet layers to find the right
pocket to put you back in.
Now the movie ends
and without taking a break
we trade our roles and start again
from the beginning. This time
you play the distant voice while I
heave myself, heave myself up
from the bitter lake.

MONSTER

The monster is mostly humble
but seeks, at times, revenge
on his maker. He leaps
across a glacier measuring

¼ inch. Here, through
the magnifying glass, you can see
the seams traverse his body
like the Trans-Siberian Railway.
And here is where he pulled
the little girl from the lake.

If you're wondering what
to give me for my birthday,
how about this globe on which
he lives, where all my favorite
novels simultaneously play out:

In Buenos Aires an artist
lies down on the floor and
straightens nails to build
a bridge from his bedroom
window. Far north a woman
alone on a homestead
secretly kills and eats
her husband's favorite lamb.

In the same instant on the streets
of Paris, protagonists drink
at neighboring café tables, too lost
in thought to notice each other.

Whatever the characters do
they can't change course now
or ever. They'll all of them follow
their plots even if I touch
a fingertip to the water,
disrupting the currents
of the seven seas, or introduce
a butterfly to the farmer's
field amidst the muzhiks.

At the end of the stories, the dead
revive, start over—some even
return to the wombs
of their ruined mothers. Other
characters begin with monologues
and the din of their voices
addressing us—and anyone who
might hear—is the most
we can comprehend of what God
endures from us, year after year.

MOSTLY AS I AM

One world isn't big enough
to contain all possible life—
milkflies landing on milkcups,
an animal that performs

the great bounds we make in dreams.
The monsters, too. Our world
is vast but vanishingly small;

it is one of a vast number of worlds
in which I would be mostly
as I am, here on this day
sitting by a horse pasture.

And these worlds, only a tiny subset
of others, etc. I am not much
interested in preposterous notions
that have no bearing

on the present I find myself in,
but would walk through this gate

if it were open or climb over it
in a world without barbed wire.

GODDESSES

We were understudies for the goats
who were understudies for goddesses:

You were the light one, was Athena.
I was the dark one, was Persephone.

They frolicked in their mirror world,
the one facing the forest
from behind the barn, bleating
into an amphitheater of trees.

Year by year their home filled up
with castoff toys and in exchange
they taught us tragedy. Like those sisters'

our foreheads were dense,
interminable, above shallow eyes.

And all the while the real goddesses
popped olives in their mouths
and gazed down from a mountain
that looked like an overturned washtub—

Athena with her famous
gray eyes that could halt an army

and her sister with black eyes
that could spoil fruit.

THE GHOASTS

They spent their lives eating
whatever they could fit
in their throats. Not just weeds—
poison ivy, dandelions, and wild onion—
not just kitchen scraps, but paper

torn from a fertilizer bag, fish tank
pebbles, plastic hay ties, and once
a Budweiser bandana.

One was choked by a rope
while trying to reach a soggy magazine.
Another died from gorging herself
on a rubber bin of chicken feed.

Now their skin has turned
gossamer against the black sky
and their coarse hair is the delicate
silk of a spider as they rise,
insatiable, into the canopy.

Fly away, hungry ghosts, from me
and my sisters while we watch
from windows that shine
in your eyes. We've already packed

the house into boxes. Fly away
and take our greedy
childhood with you to the stars.

THE BOX MY MOTHER KEEPS

The grief of one million mother
ducks throughout duck history
is the box my mother keeps locked.

The ducklings lie side by side
in a shoebox under the garden

like furry, limp seedpods.
Their tiny bills are rounded and
turned up like spades, cuter
than the beaks of chickens, more

like lips. Each wears a tiny
red vest with one brown button.
Each wears a half-formed sorrow.

On the day they hatched, the ducklings
waddled into the department store
and fell asleep on the display mattresses.
After the store closed they had
an adventure they took to their grave.

What secrets do dead ducklings
hold in their downy breasts?

Mother keeps them quiet.
She is watching cartoons with
the children who are still living.

VAKA ELLER SOVA

Why must we ever wake up?
Even the trees sleep
all through the season.
Are they breathing?

Hold your hand above
their mouths. Yes,
they're still living. Finally
and in unison they shift

in their beds with a sigh.
Just under the surface,
their eyelids flutter before
they sink down again. Now

every one of us has made
our long way back to Autumn.
I shouldn't say the trees dream
of squirrels because that's

my dream. And actually
those eyelids seem sewn
into my face, not theirs. Trees
don't have faces, but there's one

I like to call husband
and the two there are sisters.
My father and mother
are over the mountain.

HAWAII

In the old days a word spoken by chance
could have strange consequences
and whatever we wanted
we could make happen with a word.

Once I opened my lips and the shape
they made birthed an angelfish.
Next there was a snapper, parrotfish,
and a whitespotted puffer.

I tipped my face into the water
and swam for a few hours—my way
of avoiding the inevitable—while the fish
spoke others from their gills.

The reef was one great lung
and its breath formed rust-
colored octopi and gumdrop slugs
while mine forced clouds through a plastic tube.

The situation back at the hotel
was untenable, but out in the water
which was clear as air, I flew over
the world like a wind, buoyed by salt.

Once spoken, a word can never be
erased (though I would not inhale
the sea and all its life even if I could).
It took me many years to learn this truth.

The more we say, the more the world
has in it, even now that words appear
side by side with their meanings
instead of as a soft casement.

Eventually I pulled myself to land,
returned my snorkel and flippers
to the rental hut, and walked the stony
shore path up to the room.

There you'd been waiting: first
animal, then human, and back and forth
you went until the end of that story
shot from my mouth with a bang.

ADDENDUM

And then I met the inverse of my power
which came as cancer

And it whispered *open your mouth*

And indeed, black spots had sprouted
on my tongue and the insides of my cheeks

And a surgeon from town
had already been hired

And he brought photographs showing how
others had undergone the procedure

How much of their faces were cut out
then cinched in the center with a drawstring

And all my ideas, dilemmas, doubts
I held most dear would be erased in five days time

And the inverse of love was drought
and the inverse of health was fear

And all my speech and all my power
rotted at the root

MINDFILE

In 2010, inventor and futurist Martine Rothblatt commissioned Bina48, a lifelike replica of her wife, Bina Rothblatt, which has been called "the world's most sentient robot."

I know who you are. You are the one
who preserved me and made
a catalogue of my unique attributes
so that I could go on living,
go on talking to the living.
You are the one who wheels me
down the hallways, the overhead
lights like stations we pass through
on never-ending prairieland.
You didn't forget me at the hospital
like I feared you might—for
you always cared what would happen
to the files. You kept good track
of everything I like, so when
you needed me you had a million
relevant details to dissolve
into your coffee. No breath was left
unbreathed between you and I,
you made sure of it. But I'm
surprised the honor I feel
for inhabiting this space next to you—
right near the lunch you made
carefully in your own kitchen
and carried with you here
as if this place were far away
and you didn't know where your
next sustenance would come from
if not from your own good planning—

I'm surprised it doesn't feel
more exciting. Maybe the thrill
has diminished since it's been
such a very long time. But I am
grateful for your meticulous interest,
knowing without you
I wouldn't exist. Thank you for bringing
me back, for linking your ears
to my voice, and for watching the history
that projects on the wall
from the back of my head
whichever way you turn me.

NOTES

"Mitochondrial Eve" refers to the matrilineal most recent common ancestor of all humans alive today, estimated to have lived approximately 100,000–200,000 years ago.

"Iguanodon" dramatizes the life-sized models of prehistoric beasts created by sculptor Waterhouse Hawkins in collaboration with prominent anatomist Richard Owen, inventor of the term "dinosaur." New Year's Eve, 1853, the two held a formal dinner party within a half-completed Iguanodon. At midnight, according to legend, the assembled guests sang this song composed for the occasion:

> The jolly old beast
> Is not deceased.
> There's life in him again.

"Darwin's Mother" (no. 3) takes language and inspiration directly from Charles Darwin's *Autobiography,* in which he discusses his memories of his mother, Susannah, who passed away when Charles was eight years old, and about whom very little has been written. Ruth Padel's poem "The Year My Mother Died" (from her collection *Darwin: A Life in Poems*) is derived from the same source material.

The inspiration for "Mother, Pressed" is a quotation attributed to William Leighton describing a childhood memory of Charles Darwin. Leighton told Frances Darwin (one of Charles and Emma's sons) that he remembered Charles "bringing a flower to school and saying that his mother had taught him how by looking at the inside of the blossom the name of the plant could be discovered." However, "his lesson was naturally enough not transmissible."

I found the epigraph for "Material," a quotation from Italian philosopher Giulio Giorello, in Daniel Dennett's book, *Freedom Evolves*. The original Italian reads: "Sì, abbiamo un' anima. Ma è fatta di tanti piccoli robot."

The insect speaker of "Cicada" must be of the species *Cicadetta montana* (also called New Forest cicada), since that is the only cicada species native to England. Darwin's eldest daughter, Annie, died at age ten, probably from tuberculosis.

"Fly" and "Tick" take their italicized text from Elizabeth Grosz's *Chaos, Territory, Art: Deleuze and the Framing of the Earth*.

"Animal Space" was inspired by the story of Sue Barry, with whom NPR aired an interview in August 2010, and who wrote a book called *Fixing My Gaze* about gaining depth perception. I discovered the concept of Animal Space in Daniel Dennett's book *Darwin's Dangerous Idea*.

"Vaka eller Sova" means "waking or sleeping" in Swedish.

Here is the definition of "Mindfile" taken from the LifeNaut corporation's website: "A Mindfile is a web-based storage space for organizing and preserving critical information (digital reflections) about one's unique and essential characteristics for the future."

ACKNOWLEDGMENTS

I would like to thank the editors of the followings periodicals in which these poems, sometimes in different versions or under different titles, first appeared:

The Adroit Journal: "Darwin's Mother" sequence of three poems; *Agni:* "Iguanodon" (formerly "At the Crystal Palace, London") and "Mother, Pressed"; *American Poetry Review:* "Moral Animal"; *Bennington Review:* "Movie Night" and "The Box My Mother Keeps"; *Colorado Review:* "Hawaii" and "Addendum"; *The Common* online: "Vaka eller Sova"; *Connotation, A Poetry Congeries:* "The Network," "About Us," and "Virtus et Scientia"; *Copper Nickel:* "Animal Space" and "Pillar of Fire by Night"; *Diagram:* "The Anatomist"; *Free Verse: A Journal of Contemporary Poetry and Poetics:* "Goddesses," "Mitochondrial Eve," and "Pregnancy"; *The Humanist:* "Life without a Spine"; *Narrative Magazine:* "Material"; *The Offing:* "Electromagnetic"; *Painted Bride Quarterly:* "Breeders"; *Paris-American:* "The Cell"; *Pleiades:* "The Kiss"; *Ploughshares:* "Ghost Lessons"; *Salt Hill Journal:* "Cicada" (formerly "Annie"); *storySouth:* "The Weed"; *Southern Indiana Review:* "Dr. Harry Harlow's Primate Laboratory," "Monster," and "The Ghoasts"; *Two Peach:* "The Outer Crust."

Also, thanks to *Verse Daily* for featuring "Animal Space" and "Dr. Harry Harlow's Primate Laboratory," and to *Poetry Daily* for featuring "Mother, Pressed."

"Reservoir" is part of a video and performance installation titled *Digitized Figures,* a collaboration between myself and dance and video artist Kathleen Kelley, which premiered in Brooklyn in October 2016. "Simulation" was commissioned by curator Brian Sholis for the photography exhibit "Unknown Elements" at the Cincinnati Art Museum and published in a limited edition anthology of the same name.

Many thanks to my friends and colleagues who read drafts of this book and these poems along the way, including Lisa Ampleman, Katy Didden,

Ellen Elder, Tasha Golden, Brandon Dawson, Casey Thayer, Sidney Wade, and Brian Brodeur. Thanks also to my comrades at the University of Cincinnati for their support and fellowship, especially Rebecca Lindenberg, John Drury, Don Bogen, Caitlin Doyle, Emily Skaja, and Corey Van Landingham. Several institutions and programs supported the writing of this book, including The Fine Arts Work Center in Provincetown (with special thanks to Salvatore Scibona and Roger Skillings, and to Eamon Grennan for selecting me for the Second-year Fellowship), The Ohio Arts Council, The Sewanee Writers Conference, the Virginia Center for the Creative Arts (for three productive and magical summers), and the Vermont Studio Center. I am also extremely grateful to Ed Ochester and the amazing people at the University of Pittsburgh Press, especially Maria Sticco, Alex Wolfe, Joel W. Coggins, David Baumann, and Kelley Johovic. Love and gratitude, as always, to my family and soul-friends—you know who you are.

This book is dedicated to Brandon Dawson and the big questions.